JOSH STEVE

Whispers of Serenity

Copyright © 2023 by Josh Steve

All rights reserved. No part of this publication may be reproduced, stored or transmitted in any form or by any means, electronic, mechanical, photocopying, recording, scanning, or otherwise without written permission from the publisher. It is illegal to copy this book, post it to a website, or distribute it by any other means without permission.

This novel is entirely a work of fiction. The names, characters and incidents portrayed in it are the work of the author's imagination. Any resemblance to actual persons, living or dead, events or localities is entirely coincidental.

Josh Steve asserts the moral right to be identified as the author of this work.

First edition

This book was professionally typeset on Reedsy.
Find out more at reedsy.com

Contents

The Perfect Couple	1
A Hidden Debt	5
Seeking Financial Guidance	8
A Drastic Decision	12
The Plan in Motion	16
Unexpected Windfalls	20
A Twist of Fate	24
The Hidden Legacy	28
The Moral Dilemma	32
The Unforeseen Challenge	36
The Enigmatic Visitor	40
The Quest for Answers	45

The Perfect Couple

The midday sun bathed the picturesque town of Willowbrook in a warm, golden glow. Nestled between rolling hills and a pristine river, it was the kind of place where time seemed to slow down, where life flowed as smoothly as the river's current. It was in this idyllic setting that we first meet Lily and Alex, the seemingly perfect couple.

Lily, with her long chestnut hair and eyes that sparkled like emeralds, had a smile that could light up a room. She was known around town for her infectious laughter and her knack for turning any occasion into a celebration. In her early thirties, she radiated a vibrant energy that charmed everyone she met.

Alex, on the other hand, was the quiet and steady anchor in their relationship. Tall and well-built, with sandy blonde hair and a chiseled jawline, he had a presence that commanded respect. A successful architect in his late thirties, he was meticulous in his work and known for his unwavering commitment to excellence.

Together, they were the envy of Willowbrook. Their love was the stuff of legends, the kind of love that made people believe in soulmates. They had met in college, fallen in love at first sight, and had been inseparable ever since. Their friends often joked that they were the perfect couple.

But beneath the surface of their storybook romance, there were cracks beginning to appear, and it all revolved around a secret that had been carefully hidden from the world.

On this particular day, Lily and Alex sat in the cozy corner of their favorite coffee shop, The Riverside Café. It was a quaint little place with mismatched chairs and a comforting aroma of freshly baked pastries. The café overlooked the river, and it was their sanctuary—a place where they could escape the demands of daily life.

Lily sipped her cappuccino and gazed out of the café's window, her thoughts a million miles away. She had been acting strangely for weeks, and Alex couldn't ignore it any longer. He studied her with concern, his coffee untouched.

"Lily," he began cautiously, "is something bothering you?"

Startled, she turned her gaze from the window to meet his concerned eyes. "Bothering me? No, everything's fine, Alex."

But it wasn't fine. Alex could see the worry lines etched on her forehead, the way she avoided his gaze. There was something she wasn't telling him, and it gnawed at his insides.

"Lily," he pressed gently, "you can tell me anything. We promised to always be honest with each other."

Lily sighed, her shoulders slumping as if a heavy burden weighed her down. She placed her coffee cup on the saucer and took a deep breath.

"Alex, there's something I need to tell you," she began, her voice quivering. "But promise me you won't be angry, okay?"

Alex nodded, his heart pounding in his chest. He couldn't imagine what could be so serious that Lily was hesitating to share.

"It's about our finances," Lily admitted, her eyes brimming with tears. "I've been keeping something from you, and it's been eating me alive."

Alex's brow furrowed. "Our finances? What are you talking about?"

Lily took another deep breath and steeled herself. "I have credit card debt, Alex. A lot of it. I didn't want to tell you because I was ashamed, but it's gotten out of control."

The weight of her confession hung in the air, suffocating the cozy atmosphere of the café. Alex felt like he'd been punched in the gut. He had never expected this revelation, and it left him reeling.

Credit card debt was a betrayal of the unspoken agreement they had always shared: to be open and honest about their financial matters. It wasn't just a financial issue; it was a breach of trust that threatened to shatter the foundation of their perfect relationship.

Alex struggled to find words, his mind racing. "How…how much debt are we talking about?"

Lily hesitated, her lower lip trembling. "It's over fifty thousand dollars, Alex. I didn't know how to tell you, and I kept thinking I could handle it on my own."

The number hung in the air like a dark cloud, casting a shadow over their relationship. Fifty thousand dollars was a substantial amount, and Alex couldn't fathom how Lily had managed to accumulate such a debt without his knowledge.

He tried to keep his voice steady as he asked, "Why didn't you come to me sooner, Lily? We're a team. We face our problems together."

Tears welled up in Lily's eyes as she replied, "I was scared, Alex. Scared of disappointing you, of ruining what we have. I thought I could fix it, but it only got worse."

The café seemed to close in around them, the sounds of clinking cups and hushed conversations fading into the background. For the first time in their relationship, there was a palpable distance between them, a breach of trust that threatened to tear them apart.

Alex knew that their perfect love story had just taken a devastating turn, and he was faced with a choice: to let this revelation destroy them or to find a way to rebuild the trust that had been shattered.

As he gazed into Lily's tear-filled eyes, he made his decision. Their journey was about to become a lot more complicated, but he was determined to navigate the storm and find a way back to the love they had always known.

Little did he know that their path forward would be fraught with twists and turns, testing the strength of their love and the depth of their commitment in ways they could never have imagined.

A Hidden Debt

The moon hung low in the night sky, casting a silvery glow over Willowbrook. It was late, and the town was asleep, unaware of the storm that was brewing in Lily and Alex's home. In their cozy bedroom, bathed in the soft light of a bedside lamp, the couple sat on opposite sides of the bed, the chasm between them widening with every passing moment.

Alex had spent the evening poring over their financial records, his face etched with a mixture of anger and disappointment. Lily's confession of her massive credit card debt had hit him like a freight train, and he couldn't shake the feeling of betrayal.

Across from him, Lily watched his every move, her heart heavy with guilt. She knew she had hurt him deeply, and she couldn't bear to see the pain in his eyes. She had never seen him like this, so distant and cold.

Finally, breaking the silence that had hung between them like a suffocating shroud, Alex spoke in a tone that sent shivers down Lily's spine. "Lily, I need you to be completely honest with me now. Is there anything else you haven't told me?"

Lily hesitated for a moment, her mind racing. She had laid her deepest secret bare, and she didn't know if she could reveal more. But the look in Alex's eyes demanded the truth, and she knew she couldn't hold back any longer.

"Yes, Alex," she admitted, her voice barely above a whisper. "There's one more thing."

Alex's jaw tightened, his patience wearing thin. "What is it?"

Tears welled up in Lily's eyes as she began to speak, her words shaky but sincere. "I've been borrowing money from my parents to make minimum payments on the credit cards. They think we're doing fine financially, and I couldn't bear to tell them the truth."

The revelation hit Alex like a second blow. He had always prided himself on being self-reliant and responsible, and now he learned that Lily had not only hidden her debt but had also been deceiving her own parents to cover it up.

His voice quivered with anger as he asked, "How much money have you borrowed from them?"

Lily wiped away a tear and whispered, "Almost twenty thousand dollars."

The room seemed to close in around them, suffocating and oppressive. The weight of Lily's secrets bore down on them both, threatening to crush their relationship. Alex stood abruptly and began to pace the room, his mind racing.

"How could you do this, Lily?" he said, his voice rising. "You've not only hidden this from me but also lied to your parents, taken advantage of their trust. Do you have any idea how much damage this has caused, not just to our finances but to our trust and our relationship?"

Lily buried her face in her hands, her sobs muffled. She knew she had made a terrible mistake, and the consequences were now unfolding before her like a nightmare.

"I'm so sorry, Alex," she choked out. "I never meant for any of this to happen. I thought I could handle it on my own, but it spiraled out of control."

Alex stopped pacing and stood by the window, looking out at the moonlit night. His anger was still palpable, but beneath it, there was a sense of helplessness. He loved Lily with all his heart, but her actions had shattered the trust they had built over years.

After a long, tense silence, he turned back to her and said, "Lily, we're going to have to face this together. We'll talk to your parents, and we'll come up with a plan to pay off this debt. But understand this: our relationship will never be the same. Trust is fragile, and you've broken it."

Lily nodded, tears streaming down her cheeks. She knew the road ahead would be difficult, filled with challenges and sacrifices. But she was willing to do whatever it took to make things right, to rebuild the love and trust that had been damaged.

As they lay in bed that night, the room heavy with the weight of their secrets and regrets, Lily and Alex faced an uncertain future. The storm had not yet passed, and they were about to embark on a journey that would test the strength of their love in ways they could never have imagined.

Little did they know that the hidden debt was just the beginning of their financial troubles, and that deeper secrets and unexpected twists awaited them in the chapters to come. The path ahead was shrouded in darkness, but they would have to find the strength to navigate it together, holding on to the hope that their love would endure.

Seeking Financial Guidance

The sun had risen over Willowbrook, bringing with it a new day and a glimmer of hope. For Lily and Alex, the night had been a restless one, filled with questions and uncertainty. But now, as the morning light streamed through their bedroom window, they knew they had to face the reality of their financial situation head-on.

Lily had barely slept, her mind racing with thoughts of the debt that had cast a shadow over their once-perfect life. She lay beside Alex, who had been awake for hours, his thoughts churning as he contemplated their next steps.

Finally, unable to bear the weight of their secrets any longer, Alex turned to Lily and said, "We need to talk to someone who can help us navigate this mess."

Lily nodded, her eyes weary but determined. "You're right, Alex. We can't do this on our own. But who can we trust with something so personal?"

Alex had been thinking about this since the previous night. He had researched financial advisors and found someone he believed could help them—a woman named Sarah Hartman, known in town for her expertise in financial planning and her reputation for discretion.

"We'll reach out to Sarah Hartman," Alex said. "She's experienced and has helped many couples in tough situations like ours. She'll be able to guide us through this."

With a heavy sigh, Lily agreed, and they decided to make the call that would change the course of their financial and personal lives.

Later that morning, as they sat in their living room, they dialed Sarah Hartman's number. The phone rang several times before a calm, reassuring voice answered on the other end.

"Hello, this is Sarah Hartman. How can I assist you today?"

Alex cleared his throat and began to explain their situation, his voice steady but tinged with desperation. "Ms. Hartman, my wife and I are facing some serious financial troubles, and we need help. We've been living with a hidden debt, and it's affecting our relationship and our lives."

Sarah listened attentively, asking probing questions to understand the extent of their financial issues. Lily's heart raced as they laid bare the details of their debt, the borrowed money from her parents, and the strain it had placed on their marriage.

After a thoughtful pause, Sarah spoke, her voice filled with empathy. "I'm sorry to hear about the challenges you're facing, but you've taken the first step by reaching out for help. I specialize in assisting couples with their financial issues, and I can assure you that you're not alone in this."

Over the next hour, they scheduled an appointment with Sarah for later that week. She requested that they gather all their financial documents and records to bring to their meeting. As they hung up the phone, a sense of relief washed over them. It was the beginning of their journey toward financial recovery.

In the days leading up to their meeting with Sarah, Lily and Alex meticulously gathered every financial statement, credit card bill, and loan document they could find. The stack of papers on their dining room table was a physical manifestation of the burden they had been carrying.

When the day finally arrived, they nervously entered Sarah Hartman's office, a well-appointed space with soft lighting and a sense of calm. She greeted them with a warm smile and invited them to sit down.

As they laid out their financial woes, Sarah nodded thoughtfully, her pen poised to take notes. "I appreciate your honesty," she said. "The path to financial recovery can be challenging, but with a clear plan and commitment, it's possible to overcome even the most daunting debt."

Sarah proceeded to outline a step-by-step plan for Lily and Alex. She emphasized the importance of open communication, creating a budget, and setting realistic financial goals. She also recommended seeking additional sources of income and exploring debt consolidation options.

As the meeting came to a close, Sarah offered a reassuring message. "Remember, this journey will test your relationship, but it can also strengthen it. Facing financial challenges together can bring you closer and help rebuild trust."

Lily and Alex left Sarah's office with a renewed sense of hope and purpose. They knew that the road ahead would be tough, but they were determined to follow her guidance and work toward a brighter financial future.

Over the weeks that followed, they diligently followed Sarah's advice. They created a budget that accounted for every penny, began paying off their credit card debt, and explored ways to increase their income. It was a grueling process, filled with sacrifices and tough decisions, but they faced it together, as a united front.

As they navigated the challenges of their financial recovery, Lily and Alex also began to rebuild the trust that had been shattered by Lily's hidden debt. They had open and honest conversations about their goals, their dreams, and their fears. They learned to lean on each other for support, finding strength in their shared determination to overcome their financial troubles.

As the days turned into weeks, and the weeks into months, a sense of hope and optimism returned to their lives. The storm of financial turmoil had not yet passed, but they were learning to weather it together, hand in hand.

Little did they know that even more significant challenges and unexpected twists awaited them in the chapters to come. The journey to financial recovery was far from over, and they would need every ounce of their love and resilience to face what lay ahead.

A Drastic Decision

Spring had arrived in Willowbrook, bringing with it a sense of renewal and hope. The town's gardens were in full bloom, and the streets were bustling with people enjoying the pleasant weather. But for Lily and Alex, the changing seasons seemed to mirror the tumultuous state of their lives.

In the cozy corner of The Riverside Café, where they had once shared laughter and dreams, Lily and Alex sat with furrowed brows and a sense of urgency. They had reached a crossroads in their journey to financial recovery, and a drastic decision loomed before them.

Sarah Hartman's financial guidance had been invaluable, helping them create a budget and a plan to pay off their credit card debt. They had made significant progress, but their debt still loomed large, and the weight of it continued to strain their relationship.

"Alex," Lily began, her voice trembling, "I've been thinking a lot about our situation. We've made progress, but it's going to take years to pay off this debt at the rate we're going."

Alex nodded, his gaze fixed on the cup of coffee before him. He had been grappling with the same thoughts, knowing that their current path would test their patience and resolve to the limit.

Lily continued, her words heavy with uncertainty. "What if there's another way, a faster way to get out of this mess? What if we make a drastic decision?"

Alex finally looked up, his eyes meeting hers. He could sense the gravity of what she was suggesting. "What kind of drastic decision are you thinking, Lily?"

She took a deep breath, her fingers tapping nervously on the coffee cup. "What if we sell our house? It's our most significant asset, and if we sell it, we could use the proceeds to pay off a significant portion of our debt. We could downsize, live more modestly, and start fresh."

The idea hung in the air between them, both of them acutely aware of the implications. Their house was more than just a structure; it was a symbol of their life together, a place filled with memories and dreams.

Alex's mind raced, weighing the pros and cons. On one hand, selling their house could provide much-needed relief from their debt and a fresh start. On the other hand, it meant uprooting their lives, leaving behind a home they had poured their hearts into.

"Lily," he said slowly, "selling our house is a significant step. It's not something we should take lightly. We'd have to find a new place to live, and it would mean saying goodbye to the life we've built here."

Tears welled up in Lily's eyes as she replied, "I know, Alex, but we're drowning in this debt. It's straining our relationship, and I can't bear to see you so stressed all the time. We need a solution, and this might be our best chance to start over."

As they sat in the café, the weight of their decision hung heavy over them. It was a choice that could redefine their future, a leap into the unknown. They had built their perfect life in Willowbrook, and the thought of leaving it behind was both terrifying and liberating.

Over the next few weeks, Lily and Alex carefully weighed their options. They consulted with a real estate agent to understand the value of their home and explored potential new living arrangements. They spent sleepless nights discussing the potential consequences of their decision, both financial and emotional.

The more they delved into the details, the clearer their path became. Selling their house was not just a drastic decision; it was a lifeline, a chance to break free from the suffocating grip of debt and rebuild their lives on their terms.

As they prepared to put their house on the market, the town of Willowbrook seemed to hold its breath, unaware of the monumental choice that Lily and Alex were about to make. The decision to sell their home was a closely guarded secret, known only to a few trusted friends who had supported them through their financial struggles.

The day the "For Sale" sign was placed in front of their house, the reality of their decision hit them like a tidal wave. They stood on the porch, hand in hand, gazing at the place that had been their sanctuary for years. It was a bittersweet moment, a farewell to a chapter of their lives that was coming to an end.

As potential buyers visited their home and offers began to pour in, the suspense in their lives reached a fever pitch. Each offer was a potential lifeline, a chance to wipe away their debt and start fresh. But it also meant leaving behind the comfort and familiarity of Willowbrook, the town they had called home for so long.

In the midst of the whirlwind of showings and negotiations, Lily and Alex clung to each other, their love and determination to overcome their financial troubles stronger than ever. They knew that the path ahead was uncertain, that their journey was far from over, but they were willing to take the leap together, into the unknown.

Little did they know that their decision to sell their house would set in motion a chain of events that would challenge their resolve and test the depth of their love in ways they could never have imagined. The suspense of their story was far from over, and the pages of their future were blank, waiting to be written.

The Plan in Motion

The sun hung low in the sky, casting long shadows across the front yard of Lily and Alex's house. It was a warm summer afternoon, and the air was filled with the scent of freshly cut grass. But inside the house, tension hung in the air like a heavy fog.

Boxes were scattered throughout the living room, and the walls that had once held cherished family photos were now bare. Lily and Alex were in the midst of packing up their home, preparing to say goodbye to the life they had known for so long.

The decision to sell their house had been a difficult one, but it was a step they had taken together in the hope of escaping the suffocating grip of debt. They had received an offer that would cover their outstanding credit card debt and provide a fresh start, but it meant leaving behind the comfort and familiarity of Willowbrook.

As they carefully wrapped their belongings and placed them in boxes, the weight of their decision pressed upon them. The future was uncertain, and the town that had been their sanctuary was about to become a memory.

Lily sighed as she packed away a stack of photo albums, each one filled with snapshots of their life together. "It's hard to believe we're leaving all this behind," she said, her voice tinged with sadness.

Alex nodded, his face reflecting the same mix of emotions. "I know, Lily. But it's the right decision for us. We'll find a new place to call home, and we'll start fresh without the burden of debt."

The days leading up to their move had been a whirlwind of activity. They had accepted the offer on their house and found a smaller, more affordable apartment in a neighboring town. It was a practical choice, one that would allow them to live within their means and focus on rebuilding their financial stability.

But as the moving day drew closer, the reality of their decision settled in. They were leaving behind not just a house but the life they had built in Willowbrook—the friends, the community, and the memories that had defined their existence.

On the eve of their departure, Lily and Alex sat on the porch, gazing out at the familiar streets bathed in the soft glow of the setting sun. They held each other's hands, finding solace in their shared determination to face the future together.

As the sky darkened and the first stars appeared, Lily spoke softly, her voice filled with hope. "Tomorrow is the start of a new chapter, Alex. We're leaving behind our financial troubles and embracing a fresh start."

Alex squeezed her hand, his eyes filled with love and gratitude. "I'm proud of us, Lily. We're taking control of our future, and we'll overcome whatever challenges come our way."

The moving truck arrived early the next morning, its engine rumbling as it pulled up to the curb. Lily and Alex watched as the movers loaded their belongings onto the truck, each item representing a piece of their past.

As they drove away from their house for the last time, a sense of nostalgia washed over them. The streets of Willowbrook disappeared in the rearview mirror, and their journey into the unknown began.

Their new apartment was smaller but cozy, a fresh canvas upon which to paint the next chapter of their lives. They unpacked their belongings, arranging furniture and hanging photos on the walls to make the space feel like home. It was a modest beginning, but it held the promise of a debt-free future.

In the weeks that followed, Lily and Alex settled into their new routine. They budgeted carefully, cutting unnecessary expenses and living within their means. The weight of debt had lifted, replaced by a sense of freedom and possibility.

But the journey to financial recovery was far from over. The sacrifices they had made to sell their house and downsize were just the beginning. They knew that the road ahead would be filled with challenges and uncertainties, but they were determined to face them head-on, together.

One evening, as they sat on their new balcony, sipping tea and watching the sun dip below the horizon, Lily turned to Alex with a smile. "You know, Alex, this may not be the life we had planned, but it's our life, and we're in control of it."

Alex nodded, his heart filled with gratitude for the woman beside him. "You're right, Lily. Our journey may have taken an unexpected turn, but we're stronger because of it. And no matter what lies ahead, we'll face it together."

As they looked out at the world bathed in the warm hues of twilight, Lily and Alex knew that their story was far from over. The suspense of their lives had brought them to this moment, a moment of resilience and hope, and they were ready to embrace whatever challenges the future held.

Little did they know that unexpected twists and unforeseen trials awaited them in the chapters to come. Their path to financial recovery was a winding one, but they were determined to navigate it together, with love as their compass and hope as their guiding star.

Unexpected Windfalls

The town of Willowbrook had changed since Lily and Alex had left. It was a place they once called home, but now, it felt like a distant memory. Their new life in the neighboring town was becoming routine, a rhythm of work and budgeting, as they strived to rebuild their financial stability.

As the seasons shifted, Willowbrook was preparing for its annual summer festival, a vibrant celebration that drew visitors from all around. It was a time of colorful parades, lively street performances, and the sweet aroma of cotton candy wafting through the air.

Lily and Alex had always loved the festival, and it had been a tradition for them to attend every year. But this year was different. Their financial situation had forced them to cut back on discretionary spending, and attending the festival seemed like an extravagance they couldn't afford.

One evening, as they sat on their modest balcony overlooking the town, Lily sighed, her eyes fixed on the twinkling lights of the festival in the distance. "I miss those summer nights in Willowbrook, Alex, the festival, and the sense of community."

Alex nodded, his gaze also drawn to the distant lights. "I miss it too, Lily. But we made a commitment to get our finances in order, and that means making sacrifices."

As they spoke, a warm breeze carried the distant sounds of laughter and music, a reminder of the joyous celebration taking place just beyond their reach. It was a bittersweet moment, a reminder of the life they had left behind.

The next morning, as they sipped their morning coffee, Lily noticed a letter in the mail that stood out from the usual bills and advertisements. It was a thick, cream-colored envelope with an elegant seal bearing the town's emblem. Intrigued, she opened it and began to read.

"Alex," she said, her voice tinged with excitement, "you won't believe this. It's an invitation to the Willowbrook Summer Festival Gala."

Alex raised an eyebrow, puzzled. "A gala? We've never been invited to that before. How did we get on the guest list?"

Lily continued reading the letter, her eyes widening with surprise. "It says here that we've been selected as the recipients of this year's 'Community Spirit Award' for our years of involvement in the town and our commitment to helping others."

Alex couldn't believe it. They had never sought recognition for their contributions to the community; they had simply done what they felt was right. To be honored in this way was unexpected and humbling.

As they prepared for the gala, Lily and Alex couldn't help but feel a mix of excitement and trepidation. It was an opportunity to return to Willowbrook, to reconnect with friends and acquaintances, and to relive the festivities they had missed so much.

The gala was held in the grand ballroom of Willowbrook's historic town hall, a beautiful space adorned with crystal chandeliers and draped in lush, midnight blue fabric. The room buzzed with the energy of the town's most prominent residents, and Lily and Alex felt a sense of belonging amid the familiar faces.

They were dressed in their finest attire, Lily in a flowing gown that shimmered like moonlight, and Alex in a well-tailored suit that accentuated his presence. As they mingled with the guests, they received warm congratulations for their award, and it was clear that the town held them in high regard.

The evening was filled with laughter and dancing, the strains of a live jazz band filling the air. Lily and Alex felt like they were in a dream, surrounded by the beauty and opulence of the gala. It was a stark contrast to their new life in the neighboring town, and for a moment, they allowed themselves to forget their financial troubles.

As the night wore on, the mayor of Willowbrook took the stage to present the Community Spirit Award. Lily and Alex watched with bated breath, their hearts pounding in anticipation.

"The recipients of this year's award have shown unwavering dedication to our beloved town," the mayor announced. "They have demonstrated the true meaning of community spirit through their selfless actions and commitment to helping others."

The mayor's words resonated with the crowd, and all eyes turned to Lily and Alex as they were called to the stage to receive the award. As they stood before the applauding audience, a sense of pride and gratitude washed over them.

In her acceptance speech, Lily spoke from the heart. "We are deeply honored to receive this award, but we want to emphasize that our actions were never motivated by recognition. We believe in the strength of our community, and we will continue to support it in any way we can."

The applause was thunderous, and Lily and Alex returned to their seats, their hearts filled with a sense of purpose. The award was a reminder that, despite their financial challenges, they still had the power to make a positive impact on the lives of others.

As the gala continued, Lily and Alex enjoyed the festivities and the company of friends they hadn't seen in months. It was a night filled with joy and camaraderie, a glimpse into the life they had once known.

But as the clock neared midnight, the reality of their new life began to creep back in. They knew they couldn't stay at the gala forever, and the challenges of their financial journey awaited them outside the ballroom doors.

As they left the grand event, the night was cool and filled with the fragrance of summer flowers. Lily and Alex walked hand in hand through the quiet streets of Willowbrook, the echoes of the gala fading behind them.

It had been a night of unexpected windfalls, of recognition and celebration. But they knew that the true rewards in life were not found in awards or galas; they were found in the strength of their love and their commitment to facing their challenges together.

Little did they know that even more unexpected twists and turns awaited them in the chapters to come, as their journey to financial recovery continued. The suspense of their story was far from over, and the pages of their future held secrets they could never have imagined.

A Twist of Fate

Months had passed since Lily and Alex's memorable night at the Willowbrook Summer Festival Gala. The town that had once been their home now felt like a distant memory, as they settled into their new life in the neighboring town, adjusting to a simpler and more budget-conscious lifestyle.

Their financial journey had been marked by determination and resilience, and they had made significant progress in paying off their debt. But the path to financial stability was long and challenging, and the weight of their past financial mistakes continued to linger.

One crisp autumn morning, as Lily and Alex sipped coffee at their small kitchen table, a knock on the door disrupted their routine. It was an unexpected visitor—a man in his forties with a warm smile and an air of authority. He introduced himself as William Thornton, an attorney from Willowbrook.

"Good morning," William began, his tone polite but businesslike. "I hope I'm not intruding. I've been tasked with executing the will of a late resident of Willowbrook, and I have some important information to share."

Lily and Alex exchanged puzzled glances, neither of them recognizing the attorney or knowing of any connections to Willowbrook that would involve a will. They invited him in, and he explained the purpose of his visit.

"I represent the estate of Mr. Robert Thompson," William continued. "He was a longtime resident of Willowbrook and a well-known philanthropist. In his will, he left a significant bequest to the town, as well as specific instructions for a few individuals."

Lily and Alex listened intently, still unsure of why they were involved in this matter. William reached into his briefcase and produced a sealed envelope with their names written on it.

"Mr. Thompson's will includes a bequest to you both," William said, handing the envelope to Lily. "He held your commitment to the town in high regard and wanted to recognize your contributions."

Lily and Alex exchanged bewildered glances as Lily carefully opened the envelope and read the contents. Their eyes widened in disbelief as they saw the sum mentioned—an amount that would completely wipe out their remaining debt.

"We can't accept this," Alex stammered, his voice filled with astonishment. "It's too much. We never expected anything like this."

William nodded understandingly. "I understand your hesitation, but Mr. Thompson's wishes were clear. He wanted to provide assistance to those who have shown a deep commitment to the well-being of Willowbrook."

As they continued to discuss the unexpected windfall, William explained that the funds would be used to pay off their remaining debt, and any excess would be placed in a trust for their future financial security. The weight of their past financial mistakes would finally be lifted.

Overwhelmed by gratitude, Lily and Alex accepted the bequest with a sense of awe. It was a twist of fate they could have never predicted, a lifeline that would allow them to finally put their financial troubles behind them.

As they sat in their cozy living room, the weight of debt that had loomed over them for so long began to lift. The future now held promise and financial stability, and they could finally focus on their dreams and aspirations.

In the days that followed, they paid off their remaining debt, their hearts filled with a sense of liberation. The burden they had carried for years was gone, and they felt like a weight had been lifted from their shoulders.

But the unexpected windfall also brought with it a sense of responsibility. They knew that Mr. Thompson's bequest was a testament to their commitment to the town and its community. They were determined to honor his legacy by continuing to support causes they believed in and giving back to the community that had once been their home.

As the seasons shifted and the town of Willowbrook prepared for its winter festivities, Lily and Alex felt a sense of completion and closure. They decided to return to the town they had left behind, to rekindle old friendships and share their gratitude for the generosity that had changed their lives.

The winter festival was a magical affair, with the town adorned in twinkling lights and the streets bustling with visitors. Lily and Alex attended the festival with a renewed sense of belonging, their hearts filled with warmth and appreciation for the town that had once been their sanctuary.

As they watched the snowfall, the sounds of laughter and music echoing through the night, Lily turned to Alex with a smile. "Life has a way of surprising us, doesn't it?"

Alex nodded, his gaze filled with love. "It does, Lily. And no matter what challenges we face, as long as we face them together, we can overcome anything."

The night was filled with joy and camaraderie, a celebration of the unexpected twists of fate that had brought Lily and Alex to this moment. Their journey to financial stability had been a winding one, marked by determination, sacrifice, and the kindness of a late resident who had changed their lives.

Little did they know that even more surprises and adventures awaited them in the chapters to come, as their life together continued to unfold. The suspense of their story was far from over, and the pages of their future were filled with untold secrets and possibilities.

The Hidden Legacy

Winter had settled over Willowbrook, blanketing the town in a pristine layer of snow. The streets glistened under the soft glow of streetlights, and the air was filled with the crisp scent of winter. For Lily and Alex, it was a season of reflection and gratitude.

The unexpected windfall from Mr. Thompson's bequest had changed their lives in profound ways. Their financial troubles were a distant memory, and they were now focused on building a future filled with hope and possibility.

As they settled into their cozy living room, the warmth of the fireplace and the soft hum of holiday music in the background, Lily turned to Alex with a thoughtful expression. "You know, Alex, we've been given a second chance at financial stability, and it's a gift we shouldn't take lightly."

Alex nodded, his eyes filled with determination. "You're right, Lily. We've learned from our past mistakes, and we have a responsibility to make the most of this opportunity."

With the holiday season in full swing, they decided to make a difference in the lives of others. They contributed to local charities and organized a holiday food drive, rallying the community to support those in need. It was their way of giving back and honoring the legacy of generosity that had touched their lives.

One evening, as they returned home from volunteering at a local shelter, they noticed an envelope on their doorstep. It was a simple white envelope with no return address, and it piqued their curiosity. They opened it together, revealing a handwritten note inside.

"Meet me at the old willow tree in Willowbrook Park tomorrow at noon. There's something important I need to share with you."

The message was signed with a single initial, "R."

Lily and Alex exchanged puzzled glances. They had no idea who "R" could be or what this mysterious meeting could be about. But their curiosity got the better of them, and they decided to keep the appointment.

The following day, as the clock struck noon, Lily and Alex stood beneath the towering branches of the old willow tree in Willowbrook Park. The park was a place filled with memories for them, a reminder of the town they had once called home.

As they waited, the wind rustled through the branches, sending a shiver down their spines. Minutes ticked by, and they began to wonder if the meeting had been a prank or a mistake. Just as they were about to leave, a figure emerged from the shadows.

It was a woman, her face obscured by a hood, and her voice filled with urgency. "I'm sorry to bring you here like this, but I had to be cautious. My name is Rachel, and I have something important to tell you."

Lily and Alex exchanged wary glances, unsure of what to make of this unexpected encounter. "What do you want from us, Rachel?" Alex asked, his voice tinged with suspicion.

Rachel stepped closer, her eyes filled with a mixture of fear and determination. "I knew Mr. Thompson, the philanthropist who left you the bequest. He was my uncle, and I was his only living relative."

Lily and Alex were taken aback by this revelation. Mr. Thompson had never mentioned having a niece, and they had no knowledge of his family.

Rachel continued, her voice trembling. "My uncle was a kind and generous man, but he had a secret, a hidden legacy that he couldn't bear to reveal until it was too late."

She reached into her bag and produced a weathered envelope, sealed with a wax emblem bearing the town's emblem—the same emblem that had adorned the envelope of their unexpected windfall.

"He left behind a letter, addressed to the two of you," Rachel explained. "In it, he reveals a secret that has haunted him for years, a secret that has the power to change the course of your lives."

With trembling hands, Rachel handed the sealed envelope to Lily. As she opened it, her heart pounded in anticipation of the revelation that awaited them.

The letter inside was written in Mr. Thompson's elegant hand, and as Lily began to read, her eyes widened in astonishment. The words on the page held a shocking truth, a revelation that would turn their world upside down.

In the letter, Mr. Thompson confessed to a hidden treasure, a vast fortune that he had secretly amassed over the years. It was a wealth that he had kept hidden from the world, including his own family, out of fear that it would corrupt those he loved.

He explained that the fortune was now theirs, a bequest that would provide them with financial security beyond their wildest dreams. But it came with a choice—an ethical dilemma that would test their principles and values.

As Lily and Alex listened to Rachel's explanation and read the letter, they were overwhelmed by a mix of emotions. The hidden legacy of Mr. Thompson was a revelation they could have never imagined, a twist of fate that would force them to confront their deepest convictions.

Rachel pleaded with them to consider their decision carefully, to weigh the consequences of accepting the hidden fortune and the moral implications it carried.

As they stood beneath the old willow tree, the wind whispering through the branches, Lily and Alex faced a choice that would define their future. The suspense of their story had taken an unexpected turn, and the pages of their future held secrets and dilemmas they could never have anticipated.

The Moral Dilemma

Lily and Alex sat in their living room, the letter from Mr. Thompson's hidden legacy lying on the coffee table between them. The weight of the revelation hung heavy in the air, casting a shadow over their cozy home.

The fortune detailed in the letter was staggering, a sum that could change their lives in ways they had never imagined. It was a legacy that Mr. Thompson had kept hidden out of fear that it would corrupt those he loved.

As they contemplated the moral dilemma before them, Lily spoke, her voice tinged with uncertainty. "Alex, this is an unimaginable opportunity, a chance to secure our financial future and fulfill our dreams. But it comes with a price—a choice that could test our principles."

Alex nodded, his brow furrowed with thought. "I know, Lily. Accepting this fortune would free us from financial worries, but it would also mean compromising the values we hold dear. We need to think this through carefully."

They decided to seek advice from Sarah Hartman, the financial advisor who had guided them through their journey to financial stability. Sarah was known for her wisdom and ethical principles, and they trusted her counsel.

When they met with Sarah in her office, they explained the situation and handed her the letter from Mr. Thompson. She read it carefully, her expression thoughtful, before looking up at them.

"This is a significant ethical dilemma," Sarah began, her tone measured. "Accepting this fortune would undoubtedly provide financial security and the means to fulfill your dreams. But it would also raise questions about the source of the wealth and whether it was obtained ethically."

Lily and Alex nodded, their hearts heavy with the weight of the decision before them.

Sarah continued, "Before making a choice, I would suggest investigating the source of the fortune and Mr. Thompson's motivations. It's important to understand the full picture before making a decision that could have far-reaching consequences."

They left Sarah's office with a sense of clarity and a plan to uncover the truth behind Mr. Thompson's hidden legacy. They began by researching his life, his philanthropic endeavors, and any clues that could shed light on the source of the fortune.

As they delved deeper into Mr. Thompson's past, they discovered a pattern of generosity and a dedication to supporting various charitable causes in Willowbrook. His wealth had been amassed through astute investments and shrewd business decisions, and there was no evidence of unethical practices.

They also learned about Mr. Thompson's personal struggles, his fear that the wealth he had accumulated could corrupt his loved ones, and his desire to protect them from the burdens of wealth.

The more they uncovered, the clearer the picture became. Mr. Thompson's legacy was one of generosity and a commitment to making a positive impact on the community he loved.

But the moral dilemma remained. Lily and Alex knew that accepting the fortune would mean compromising their principles, even if the source of the wealth was ethical. They had always believed in financial responsibility and self-reliance, and they questioned whether they could reconcile these values with the hidden legacy.

One evening, as they sat in front of the fireplace, the flickering flames casting dancing shadows on the walls, Lily turned to Alex with a heavy heart. "Alex, I've been thinking about our decision. As much as I'm tempted by the financial security this fortune could provide, I can't ignore the discomfort it brings."

Alex nodded in agreement, his expression pensive. "I feel the same way, Lily. We've worked hard to overcome our past financial mistakes and to build a life based on responsibility and integrity. Accepting this fortune would feel like betraying those principles."

They decided to meet with Rachel, Mr. Thompson's niece, and share their decision. They wanted her to know that they had carefully considered the offer and had chosen not to accept the hidden legacy.

When they met with Rachel in a quiet cafe in Willowbrook, they explained their choice, emphasizing their commitment to their values and the importance of financial responsibility.

Rachel listened intently, her eyes filled with understanding. "I knew my uncle's legacy came with a difficult choice," she said. "He struggled with it for years, and I believe he would respect your decision."

As they parted ways with Rachel, they felt a sense of relief and resolution. The moral dilemma had been a challenging test of their principles, but they had emerged from it with their integrity intact.

As winter turned to spring, Lily and Alex continued their journey to financial stability, no longer burdened by the weight of the hidden legacy. They knew that their decision had been the right one for them, a choice that allowed them to stay true to their values and principles.

Their life was no longer defined by financial troubles or unexpected windfalls, but by the strength of their love and their unwavering commitment to facing challenges together. The suspense of their story had reached a turning point, and the pages of their future held secrets and adventures they were eager to explore.

The Unforeseen Challenge

With the moral dilemma of Mr. Thompson's hidden legacy behind them, Lily and Alex continued to rebuild their lives in the neighboring town. Their financial stability was no longer an elusive dream but a reality they had achieved through hard work and principled choices.

As spring blossomed, they found themselves exploring new opportunities and pursuing their passions. Lily began volunteering at a local animal shelter, her love for animals reignited, and Alex took up woodworking, crafting intricate pieces in their small garage workshop.

But as the days grew longer, and the promise of summer beckoned, an unforeseen challenge loomed on the horizon. It arrived in the form of an unexpected letter that arrived one sunny afternoon.

Lily retrieved the mail from the mailbox, sifting through the envelopes, and her heart skipped a beat when she saw the return address. It was from the IRS, the Internal Revenue Service.

She opened the letter with trembling hands and began to read. Her eyes widened in shock as she absorbed the contents. It was a notice of a tax audit—a comprehensive examination of their financial records for the past three years.

"Alex!" she called out, her voice filled with alarm. "We're being audited by the IRS!"

Alex hurried into the room, his expression mirroring her concern as he read the letter. "This is unexpected," he said, his voice tight with anxiety. "We've always been diligent about our taxes. Why would they choose us for an audit?"

Lily shook her head, unable to comprehend why they were being subjected to such scrutiny. "I have no idea, Alex. But we need to gather all our financial records and be prepared for this audit."

Over the next few weeks, Lily and Alex dedicated themselves to the painstaking process of gathering and organizing their financial documents. They knew that the audit would be an arduous and invasive process, one that could potentially uncover discrepancies or errors that they were unaware of.

As the day of the audit approached, they sought advice from a tax professional to ensure they were adequately prepared. The professional reviewed their records and assured them that they had been diligent in their tax filings, making it unlikely that any major issues would arise.

But the anxiety of the impending audit continued to weigh on them. It was a cloud that hung over their lives, a source of stress and uncertainty that they couldn't escape.

The day of the audit arrived, and Lily and Alex sat nervously in a small room at the IRS office. Across from them sat an auditor, a stern-faced woman in her forties who wasted no time in getting down to business.

Over the course of several hours, the auditor meticulously reviewed their financial records, asking probing questions and scrutinizing every detail. Lily and Alex answered each question to the best of their ability, their anxiety growing with each passing minute.

As the audit neared its conclusion, the auditor looked up from her paperwork and fixed them with a penetrating gaze. "I have one final question," she said. "Did you receive any unexpected windfalls or significant gifts in the past few years?"

Lily and Alex exchanged a glance, their hearts sinking. They knew that the audit had likely uncovered the bequest from Mr. Thompson, a windfall they had chosen not to accept. They had disclosed the gift in their tax filings, but the decision not to accept it had likely raised red flags.

Lily took a deep breath and explained the situation, detailing their choice to decline the fortune and their commitment to their principles. The auditor listened carefully, her expression inscrutable.

After what felt like an eternity, the auditor closed her file and leaned back in her chair. "I understand your decision," she said, her tone softer than before. "While it's unusual to decline a significant gift, it appears that you have acted in accordance with your principles. The audit is complete, and there are no issues with your tax filings."

Relief washed over Lily and Alex, their anxiety giving way to gratitude. They had passed the audit without any major issues, and their financial integrity remained intact.

As they left the IRS office, the weight that had hung over them for weeks began to lift. They knew that the audit had been a challenging and unexpected ordeal, but it had also reaffirmed their commitment to financial responsibility and their unwavering dedication to their principles.

As summer arrived, and the town came alive with festivals and outdoor activities, Lily and Alex felt a renewed sense of freedom. The audit had been an unforeseen challenge, but they had faced it together, emerging stronger and more resilient.

Their journey to financial stability was far from over, and they knew that unexpected twists and turns would continue to shape their path. But with love as their anchor and their principles as their guide, they were ready to face whatever challenges the future held.

Little did they know that even more surprises and adventures awaited them in the chapters to come, as their life together continued to unfold. The suspense of their story was far from over, and the pages of their future were filled with untold secrets and possibilities.

The Enigmatic Visitor

Summer was in full bloom in the neighboring town, and Lily and Alex had embraced the warmth and vibrancy of the season. The challenges of the IRS audit had faded into the past, and their lives had settled into a comfortable rhythm of work, community involvement, and moments of leisure.

One sunny afternoon, as they strolled through a local farmers' market, their hands entwined, a sense of contentment washed over them. The market was bustling with activity, vendors offering fresh produce, artisanal goods, and colorful blooms.

As they perused the market stalls, they were drawn to a particularly charming booth adorned with handcrafted jewelry. The pieces on display were exquisite, each one a work of art in its own right.

A woman in her fifties stood behind the booth, her warm smile inviting them to explore her creations. Her eyes sparkled with an air of mystery, and she exuded an aura of quiet wisdom.

"Welcome," she greeted them in a soft, melodic voice. "I'm Amelia. Please feel free to take a closer look at my jewelry."

Lily and Alex exchanged glances, captivated by the beauty of the jewelry.

They began to examine the pieces, each one more intricate and captivating than the last.

Amelia watched them with a knowing smile, as if she could sense their appreciation for her craftsmanship. "I put my heart and soul into each piece," she said. "Every gemstone, every bead, has its own story to tell."

As they admired the jewelry, Lily noticed a pendant that stood out—a delicate silver pendant adorned with a deep blue sapphire. It was a stunning piece, the sapphire shimmering with an inner light.

Amelia noticed Lily's interest and gently handed her the pendant. "That's a special piece," she said. "It's said to bring clarity and guidance to those who wear it. It's called the 'Sapphire of Serenity.'"

Lily held the pendant in her hand, feeling an inexplicable connection to it. It was as if the sapphire whispered to her, beckoning her to embrace its serenity.

Alex, too, was drawn to a particular piece—a set of cufflinks made from polished tiger's eye gemstones. The swirling patterns within the stones seemed to hold a mesmerizing depth.

Amelia smiled knowingly as Alex examined the cufflinks. "Tiger's eye is a stone of protection and courage," she explained. "It's believed to bring balance and strength to those who wear it."

After some contemplation, Lily and Alex decided to purchase the pendant and the cufflinks, drawn not only to the beauty of the jewelry but also to the aura of mystery that surrounded Amelia and her creations.

As they left the farmers' market, the pendant and cufflinks tucked safely in a small velvet box, Lily couldn't shake the feeling that there was more to Amelia than met the eye. She seemed to carry a secret, an enigmatic presence that had left an indelible mark on their minds.

Over the next few weeks, as they wore their respective pieces of jewelry, they began to notice subtle changes in their lives. Lily found herself feeling calmer and more centered, her decision-making clearer than ever before. Alex, too, felt a newfound sense of confidence and resilience in the face of challenges.

They couldn't help but wonder if the jewelry was more than just adornments—whether it held a deeper significance or power. It was a thought they shared in hushed conversations, as if speaking it aloud might reveal a hidden truth.

One evening, as they sat on their porch, the pendant and cufflinks glinting in the soft glow of twilight, a knock on the door interrupted their reverie. It was an unexpected visitor—an elderly man with a weathered face and a twinkle in his eye.

"Good evening," the man greeted them with a warm smile. "My name is Samuel. I couldn't help but notice the jewelry you've been wearing."

Lily and Alex exchanged puzzled glances. The jewelry had garnered attention before, but this encounter felt different, as if Samuel held a deeper understanding.

Samuel continued, "I see you have the 'Sapphire of Serenity' and the tiger's eye cufflinks. Those are powerful pieces, with their own unique stories."

Lily and Alex invited Samuel in, and he explained that he was a collector of rare and mystical artifacts, each with its own history and significance. He had spent a lifetime searching for objects of power and significance, and he believed that the jewelry they wore was more than mere adornments.

He shared stories of gemstones and talismans, each with its own unique properties and abilities. The 'Sapphire of Serenity,' he explained, was believed to bring clarity and guidance to those who wore it, while the tiger's eye cufflinks were associated with courage and protection.

As Samuel spoke, Lily and Alex felt a sense of wonder and intrigue. It was as if they had stumbled upon a hidden world of mysteries and ancient wisdom, a world they had never imagined.

Samuel's eyes twinkled as he spoke of the jewelry's potential, but he also warned of the responsibility that came with their newfound power. "These artifacts can

be a source of great strength, but they must be wielded with wisdom and integrity. Their true power lies in the intentions of those who wear them."

As they listened to Samuel's words, Lily and Alex couldn't help but reflect on the choices they had made in their journey to financial stability—the decision to decline Mr. Thompson's hidden legacy, the principles they had upheld, and the values that guided their lives.

Samuel's visit left them with a sense of awe and reverence for the jewelry they wore. It was a reminder that there were mysteries in the world beyond their understanding, and that the choices they made had the power to shape their destiny.

As summer continued to unfold, and the town buzzed with the energy of festivals and outdoor gatherings, Lily and Alex embraced the newfound wisdom and potential of their jewelry. The enigmatic visitor had opened their eyes to a world of possibilities, and they were ready to face whatever challenges and adventures lay ahead.

Little did they know that even more surprises and mysteries awaited them in the chapters to come, as their life together continued to unfold. The suspense of their story was far from over, and the pages of their future were filled with untold secrets and journeys of discovery.

The Quest for Answers

The summer sun bathed the neighboring town in warmth and golden light, casting long shadows across the streets. Lily and Alex had settled into a sense of equilibrium, their lives filled with work, community involvement, and the intriguing jewelry they wore.

The pendant, known as the 'Sapphire of Serenity,' and the cufflinks crafted from polished tiger's eye gemstones had become more than just adornments. They seemed to possess an otherworldly quality, influencing their thoughts, actions, and the choices they made.

As the days passed, Lily found herself drawn to the pendant, its deep blue sapphire seeming to hold a world of wisdom within its facets. It brought her a sense of serenity and clarity that guided her decisions and actions.

Alex, on the other hand, often touched the cufflinks, the swirling patterns of the tiger's eye stones grounding him and infusing him with courage in the face of adversity. It was as if the jewelry had become an extension of themselves, an ethereal connection to a hidden world of possibilities.

One evening, as they sat on their porch, watching the stars twinkle in the night sky, Lily turned to Alex with a sense of wonder. "Do you ever feel like there's more to these pieces of jewelry than meets the eye? Like they hold a secret we've yet to uncover?"

Alex nodded, his gaze fixed on the cufflinks. "I can't deny that there's something extraordinary about them. They've changed us, Lily, made us better in some way. But what is their true purpose? And who is the enigmatic Amelia who crafted them?"

Lily's thoughts mirrored Alex's, and together, they decided to embark on a quest for answers. They were determined to uncover the mysteries surrounding the jewelry and the enigmatic artisan who had created them.

Their journey began with a search for information about Amelia, the jewelry maker. They scoured local directories and inquired with vendors at the farmers' market but found little information. It was as if she existed on the periphery of their town's collective consciousness, a figure shrouded in mystery.

Undeterred, they broadened their search, exploring nearby towns and communities, inquiring about anyone who matched the description of the jewelry artisan. It was a quest that took them on winding roads and through picturesque landscapes, their determination driving them forward.

Their search eventually led them to a quaint village nestled in the hills, where they encountered an elderly woman who had known Amelia. The woman's eyes held a glint of recognition as they mentioned the jewelry maker's name.

"Ah, Amelia," she said with a nostalgic smile. "She was a gifted artisan, known for her exquisite creations. But she vanished from these parts many years ago, leaving behind a legacy of beauty and mystery."

The woman shared stories of Amelia's talent and her reputation as a creator of jewelry with mystical properties. She spoke of rumors that Amelia had been on a lifelong quest to uncover the secrets of the gemstones she used in her pieces, believing that they held hidden powers.

Lily and Alex were captivated by the tales of Amelia's quest for knowledge and the belief that gemstones possessed unique qualities. It seemed that their jewelry had indeed been crafted with a purpose beyond mere adornment.

Determined to learn more, they continued their journey, tracing Amelia's footsteps to a remote cabin in the woods, where she had once lived and worked. The cabin was now abandoned, its windows covered in ivy, but it held clues to Amelia's fascination with gemstones and her relentless pursuit of knowledge.

As they explored the cabin, they discovered journals filled with sketches, notes, and observations about gemstones and their properties. It was as if Amelia had been on a quest to unlock the secrets of the jewelry she created, seeking a deeper understanding of their potential.

One entry in particular caught their attention—an intricate sketch of the 'Sapphire of Serenity' and the tiger's eye cufflinks, accompanied by cryptic symbols and annotations. It was clear that Amelia had believed these pieces to be more than just jewelry—they were artifacts with a purpose.

Their quest for answers had unearthed a wealth of information about Amelia and her belief in the jewelry's mystical properties. It was a revelation that left Lily and Alex with a sense of awe and curiosity, eager to explore the jewelry's potential.

As they left the cabin, the sun dipped below the horizon, casting long shadows in the fading light. They knew that their journey was far from over, that the mysteries of the jewelry and their connection to Amelia held secrets yet to be uncovered.

With newfound determination, they returned to their home in the neighboring town, ready to embrace the enigmatic world of gemstones and their jewelry's hidden powers. The suspense of their story had deepened, and the pages of their future were filled with untold secrets and the promise of discovery.

Little did they know that even more surprises and revelations awaited them in the chapters to come, as their life together continued to unfold. The quest for answers had only just begun, and the mysteries of the jewelry held the key to a world of possibilities they had yet to explore.

www.ingramcontent.com/pod-product-compliance
Lightning Source LLC
LaVergne TN
LVHW050027080526
838202LV00069B/6947